WAY

P9-EED-442

RACE CAR LEGENDS

The Allisons
Mario Andretti
Jeff Burton
Crashes & Collisions
Demolition Derby
Drag Racing
Dale Earnhardt
Famous Finishes
Formula One Racing
A. J. Foyt
Jeff Gordon
The History of NASCAR
Indy Car Racing
Kenny Irwin Jr.
The Jarretts
The Labonte Brothers
Lowriders
The Making of a Race Car
Mark Martin
Jeremy Mayfield
Monster Trucks & Tractors
Motorcycles
The Need for Speed
Off-Road Racing
Richard Petty
The Pit Crew
Tony Stewart
Stunt Driving
The Unsers
Rusty Wallace
Women in Racing

CHELSEA HOUSE PUBLISHERS

JEFF BURTON

June Ford

CHELSEA HOUSE PUBLISHERS
Philadelphia

Frontis: *Jeff Burton celebrates his win at the 1998 Winston Cup Series Exide 400 at the Richmond International Raceway in Richmond, Virginia.*

Produced by
21st Century Publishing and Communications, Inc.
New York, New York
http://www.21cpc.com

CHELSEA HOUSE PUBLISHERS

Production Manager: Pamela Loos
Art Director: Sara Davis
Director of Photography: Judy L. Hasday
Managing Editor: James D. Gallagher
Senior Production Editor: J. Christopher Higgins
Publishing Coordinator/Project Editor: James McAvoy

The Chelsea House World Wide Web address is
http://www.chelseahouse.com

First Printing

1 3 5 7 9 8 6 4 2

Library of Congress Cataloging-in-Publication Data

Ford, June, 1957–
   Jeff Burton / by June Ford.
      p.   cm.—(Race car legends)
   Includes bibliographical references and index.
   ISBN 0-7910-5847-6
   1. Burton, Jeff, 1967–   —Juvenile literature. 2. Automobile racing drivers—
United States—Biography—Juvenile literature. [1. Burton, Jeff, 1967–   .
2. Automobile racing drivers.] I. Title. II. Series.

GV1032.B87 F67 2000
796.72'092—dc21
[B]   00-038384
                                                                            CIP
                                                                            AC

CONTENTS

WINNING THE
POPCORN 400

The smell of seared rubber filled the air as Jeff Burton burst out of his final pit stop, barely ahead of his big brother Ward. There were 68 laps to go in the 393-lap event, and his No. 99 Roush Racing Ford was set for a short run. All during the race, he'd been successful going 40 to 50 laps between pit stops. Now Jeff was hoping the tires would hold together just a little while longer. It was a gamble to gain him the lead. If it failed, the tires would be gone, the race lost.

Problems had plagued Jeff's No. 99 since the start of the Pop Secret Popcorn 400. Part of the National Association for Stock Car Auto Racing (NASCAR) Winston Cup Series, the race took place at the famed North Carolina Speedway in Rockingham on Sunday, October 24, 1999.

Jeff had been trapped behind lapped cars all day. These cars were one or more laps behind the leader, but their position on the track was between Jeff and the lead car. He had to get past them if he

In his No. 99 Ford Taurus, Jeff Burton fought off the last-minute challenge of his brother Ward to win the 1999 Pop Secret Popcorn 400. Jeff crossed the finish line only three car lengths ahead of Ward.

were ever to take the lead.

Adding even more to his troubles were the reasons Rockingham is called "the Rock." Its abrasive asphalt surface is notorious for wearing tires down on long runs. Also, the track's 22-degree banking in turns 1 and 2 and 25-degree banking in turns 3 and 4 were giving Jeff and his team fits. His car was "loose," meaning that the rear end of the car wanted to slide toward the wall. This increased tire wear and made long runs difficult. So far, it had not been a good race for him.

Jeff Burton, 32, hadn't even been considered a contender for most of the race. But slowly and patiently he managed to weave through the lapped traffic and catch up with his brother Ward as they approached their final pit stops during a caution period.

Ward had run in one of the top three spots virtually all day. He was in the lead when the front-runners came in for their final pit stops. Four years earlier, Ward had won this race. A good pit stop and the race would once again be his. He was hungry for a win, and victory was now so close he could taste it. But then his little brother beat him out of the pits.

The caution was lifted. On the restart, Jeff Gordon tried to grab the lead by running inside of Jeff Burton, moving the No. 99 closer to the outside of the track. Gordon ran Jeff hard, and the two battled for several laps until Jeff finally cleared Gordon.

Meanwhile, Ward's Caterpillar Pontiac was stuck behind a lapped car. Jeff's big brother finally freed himself and soon closed in on No. 99, but time was running out. Jeff knew Ward's Pontiac was a better car on a long run.

If Jeff lost his lead now, he might lose the race. Keeping Ward at bay was not easy. Having to catch up with him again might be impossible.

Ward's crew thought he could win and urged him on, trying to get him past Jeff's No. 99 car. But this time, it couldn't be done. Ward held off Bobby Labonte, Dale Jarrett, and Rusty Wallace, but he failed to overtake Jeff. He missed taking the checkered flag from his younger brother by a mere 0.337 seconds—about three car lengths.

The gamble taken by Jeff and his crew chief, Frank "Frankie" Stoddard, had paid off. If Ward had either exploded out of the pit earlier than Jeff or if the race had lasted another few laps, it's likely Ward would have won. But instead, Jeff came from behind to win.

The race had only three caution flags for a

Taking a victory lap after winning the Popcorn 400, Jeff (right) passes Ward's No. 22 Caterpillar Pontiac. Although the brothers sometimes find it hard to race against each other, they don't let competition interfere with their relationship.

Jeff Burton's pit crew celebrates after the victory at Rockingham. Jeff later said that the win was a tribute to the quality of his team.

total of 18 laps, and Jeff's winning speed of 131.103 miles per hour (mph) set a track record, breaking the mark of 128.423 mph set the previous fall by Gordon.

Team effort won the hard-earned victory. "I think everybody knows we didn't have the best car all day," said Jeff. "This win is a tribute to how good a team we've got. Frank [Stoddard] made some great calls in the pits to get the car to drive the way I needed it to towards the end of the race. . . . Then we had a great pit stop to get us . . . out in front [of Ward], and I think that was important because . . . I was able to get away from him and that makes a big difference. The race was won behind that pit wall today, not behind the wheel."

Jeff and Stoddard's two-year-old team had pulled together. "Jeff and Frankie have done such a good job this year that I now expect them to make the kind of calls and to work together as they did," commented Jack Roush, owner of Roush Racing, for which Jeff pilots the No. 99 Exide Batteries Ford Taurus. "This has been a year that Frankie Stoddard and Jeff came of age. Lacking the drive train problems we had and one or two other things early in the year, Jeff and Frankie would be right there in the championship."

It was the best win the team ever had. It was also "the hardest we've ever had to work on the chassis to win a race," Jeff admitted. He added, "That last caution was definitely a blessing for us. Ward was going to check out on us. . . . Frank made the decision to go try to get everything he could on a short run. . . . We made a lot of changes to the car and got it freed up, but it was too loose on the end of a long run. . . . Ward was coming on us, he just ran out of laps."

Ward agreed. "Jeff beat us out of the pits, then I got behind some lapped traffic and he was able to get away to a big lead. If I had been on his bumper, I don't think the 99 would have won the race."

After the race, Ward had stepped out of his car and banged his fist on the spoiler. "Two hundred yards," he'd said of the distance he finished behind his brother. For the third time in 1999, the Burton brothers finished with Jeff in first and Ward in second place. Despite his frustration at losing, Ward turned to his brother, who had just pulled next to him, pointed, and smiled.

"Not only is he my brother, but we finished second to him three times," Ward reported. "We want to win a race, and hey, I don't expect him or anybody else to give it to me, but it's just the circumstance. I'm not mad at him, and his team has been doing a great job for him. One of these days I'm going to turn it around."

Jeff knows how it feels to be so close to victory and then lose. "I hate it for Ward, I really do," Jeff expressed. "I know it's a heartbreak for him. One of these days he's going to turn it around and start kicking my butt. They had a great race car. Everybody says it must be fun racing your brother. Well, it's no fun having to beat your brother. . . . I know they're real disappointed but they did a heck of a job."

Racing against his brother is not Jeff's favorite thing in life. "I feel bad that Ward didn't win this race," he said. "I know nobody believes that, but it's hard to go out there and one of your goals has to be to beat your brother. That's the hardest thing in the world."

Although 1999 appeared to have been a successful year for Jeff with 6 wins, 18 top-fives, 23 top-10s, and earnings of $5,725,399 in the Winston Cup Series, it was also disappointing. Because of three Did Not Finishes (DNFs), the team was no longer a contender for the championship, which is determined by points earned in each race.

Jeff, though, was philosophical about not being able to compete for the championship, saying, "Now, at the same time, there's positives in that. Because when you know what you've done wrong, then you can go fix it. When you don't know what you've done wrong, that's a real confusing time."

"We came into this year, based on what we had done the second half of last year with a lot of excitement," Jeff said after winning at the Rock. "This is so hard. . . . You can get your ego knocked down really quick in this business. I told Jack [Roush] yesterday, 'Have you ever been through the deal where you feel like you can't do anything right? That's where I am right now.' Then we win today. This is a fickle business."

A Go-kart Family

Jeff Burton was born on June 29, 1967, into what he describes as an average American family. Living in the rural, blue-collar town of South Boston, Virginia, his parents, John and Meredith Burton, already had two boys—six-year-old Ward and three-year-old Brian—when their third son entered the world.

One day Jeff's dad, who owned a construction company, brought home a two-seater go-kart for the three brothers. Two weeks later, eight-year-old Ward was competing at the small local go-kart track. At home, it was common to see Ward driving his two brothers around the yard, maneuvering around obstacles, as Jeff, then a toddler, bounced around in the side seat.

By the time Jeff was five, he was watching Ward and their father build go-karts. He was still so small that he stood on his tiptoes to watch them race. Eventually, all three brothers and their father were building and racing go-karts.

During the '60s and '70s, Jeff's father, John Burton, and his three sons were involved in building and racing go-karts. The family hobby would eventually lead two of the boys, Jeff and Ward, into NASCAR racing.

"When I became old enough to race, Dad quit racing because he couldn't drive and work on all the karts. I was seven at the time, and having me work on the go-karts would do more harm than good," Jeff told *NASCAR Winston Cup Illustrated.*

Unbeknownst to John Burton, that first go-kart he'd brought home for his boys had set in motion a course that would one day take two of his sons into the elite world of the NASCAR Winston Cup Series. But for now, go-karting had become the family's hobby.

"I ran go-karts for nine years and progressed up through the ranks. Brian won more state championships than any of the rest of us did," Jeff recalled.

Twice, Jeff won the Virginia State Go-kart Championship, but being a professional stock car driver was just a pipe dream.

Besides, the Burton boys weren't just interested in go-karts. They were active in school sporting events, hunting, and fishing, and they enjoyed their friends, who always seemed to be meeting at the Burtons' house, especially on Sundays—race day—to watch the races on TV.

Sometimes, John Burton would take his boys to the races at Darlington Raceway in South Carolina, as well as to Rockingham. They'd travel in a small motor home, camp out, and go to the Sunday race. At the time, Jeff idolized Cale Yarborough, who, from his first win in 1965 until he retired in 1988, won three NASCAR Winston Cup championships and had 83 career victories.

When he wasn't racing, Jeff attended Halifax County High School. He was an outstanding athlete, playing basketball and soccer and also

Jeff Burton won the Virginia State Go-kart Championship twice. But by the time he was 15, Jeff was becoming more interested in late-model stock cars.

serving as captain of the soccer team.

At 15, Jeff's interest gradually moved from go-karts to late-model stock cars on short tracks. He had begun helping a racer in his hometown work on a late-model car. When Jeff wasn't racing go-karts, he would go with the man and help with his race car.

One day after one of the races, a driver went to Victory Lane and punched out the winner. The driver was suspended for three races. Desperate for a driver for their Pure Stock entry, the suspended driver's team asked Jeff to drive. To just about everyone's surprise, Jeff won the race. A career was born.

SIBLING REV-ALRY

Jeff's surprise win wasn't without complications. He and his oldest brother, Ward, were competing in the same field. While the two young men shared a passion for cars, they were separated by many differences. With a six-year age span between them, they were not raised in the same way, and the opportunities they received to develop their driving skills were not the same either. They had different interests, and sometimes the competition between the two brothers became personal.

Ward was influenced by their grandfather's interests in wildlife, fishing, and hunting. Jeff was influenced more by their father's interest in sports. Jeff followed college basketball and is a devoted fan of the Duke Blue Devils men's basketball team. Jeff is patient. Ward is more aggressive. Jeff prefers living in a neighborhood. Ward prefers the country life. For reasons neither of them understands, they even speak with different accents.

Early on, Jeff focused on racing and convinced his

Jeff (rear) shares a passion for racing with his brother Ward. The two once fought after wrecking both their cars in a race, but the brothers now learn from each other both on and off the track.

parents to invest his freshman college savings fund in cars. Soon, the sophomore funds were invested as well. In contrast, Ward had started at the bottom of the local racing scene, driving a Volkswagen. He was lucky to have a good set of tires for each race and rarely had new tires. Jeff, on the other hand, had new tires every racing weekend. Ward later admitted that at first he'd been jealous of his youngest brother's advantages.

The brothers' introduction to street- and late-model stock car racing was far from illustrious. Both often worked all night in dingy, damp little buildings on cars. It didn't look like there was much of a future in racing, and their brother Brian had already abandoned racing for college. Jeff, who was having a tough time, recalled later that at that point he didn't think he'd ever make it on the circuit.

In 1986, at age 19, Jeff became the youngest driver in NASCAR history to win a late-model stock car race.

"I don't race because it's fun to race. I race because it's fun to beat other people at the game, whatever that game is," Jeff said. And sometimes that competitor was his brother. This left the Burton family with a problem: how to celebrate winning with one brother while comforting the other brother over his loss.

Although the two men are now supportive of each other, that was not always the case. Once in 1987, they were both racing late-model stock cars in a hometown competition. Their whole family had come to watch. With only a few laps remaining in the race, Ward was near the top of the track trying to pass a car for the lead when Jeff, who was below him, pulled under Ward.

Ward Burton (pictured here) helped his brother Jeff in his early racing days, advising him on the business side of the sport.

They both wrecked. Angry, Ward came down the track after Jeff.

"I got out of my car and went over to his car, and I had him by the neck, squeezing it. I happened to look up and I saw Daddy coming. I decided right then it was a real good time for me to get my butt to the hauler and get out of sight," Ward recalled.

"It got ugly," Jeff explained. "We got into a shoving match in front of everyone and embarrassed

Stock car drivers such as these need skill, luck, and perseverance to successfully compete in NASCAR racing. Both Burton brothers admire these qualities in each other.

our entire family, and the worst part was our mom was disappointed with us." He added, "We never, at least since we have matured as adults, have done that to each other again." Their relationship improved afterward, and they again began to learn from each other, on and off the track.

"Ward has always taken care of me. He always looked out for me," Jeff told *NASCAR Winston Cup Illustrated.* Ward had learned the importance of sponsors and the business side of racing. He helped Jeff establish himself as a driver.

On the track, they were no longer brother against brother, but competitors aiming for Victory Lane. Each admits he likes to see the other win but not at his own expense. And each says the other is his favorite driver.

Jeff won five more late-model stock division events and became the Orange County Speedway cochampion in 1987. He won seven events and was voted most popular driver at South Boston Speedway the following year. By 1989, Jeff was ready to move into the NASCAR Busch Series, Grand National Division.

Only the most elite drivers move into the NASCAR divisions. To be successful, drivers need more than skill, persistence, competitive spirit, and tenacity. They need a great car, a good pit crew, and lots of money.

For that money, they look for sponsors: a company, team, or individual to help offset the cost of cars, parts, fees, crashes, crews, salaries, travel, and other necessary expenses. It is difficult for up-and-coming drivers to find sponsors or even car owners to take them on.

"The Busch Series teaches you how to handle things," Jeff told the *Virginian-Pilot.* "When I raced Late Models at South Boston, I knew I was going to finish in the top five every week. But when I went to Busch, I didn't know if I was going to make the race."

Jeff worked and drove hard. In 1988, driving for his father, Jeff competed in five Busch Grand National races: three in a Chevrolet and two in an Oldsmobile. He didn't even place within the top 10. He ended the season 44th in points standings. But by 1989, still driving for his dad, but this time in a Pontiac, he decided to make a run at the NASCAR Busch Series Rookie of the Year award. Although he didn't make it, he finished the season with 27 starts, 2 top-5s, and 6 top-10s. He was 13th in the standings.

Jeff changed to a Buick for his 1990 season and drove for series legend Sam Ard. He won his first Busch Series in Martinsville, Virginia. In the fall race at Michigan Speedway, he took his first Busch Series pole. To win the pole, a racer must have the highest qualifying speed. At the race, the pole winner is the first car in the lineup, or grid. It's the position everyone wants. Jeff finished the year at 15th in the standings.

The following year, he drove for Bill Papke in a variety of models and won in his hometown. He finished the year 12th in the standings and had 31 starts, 1 win, 3 top-5s, 10 top-10s, and 2 poles.

In December 1992, Jeff married his junior high school sweetheart, Kim Browne. Kim tried to travel with him as often as possible and could usually be found by his side throughout the circuit. Jeff also had his best season to date in the Busch Series. He was driving for FILMAR Motorsports and drove Oldsmobiles, with the exception of one race at Dover Downs, where he drove a Ford. He won at the New Hampshire International Speedway (NHIS) in Loudon, New Hampshire. He had 31 starts, 1 win, 4 top-5s, 10 top-10s, and finished the year 9th in the standings.

But 1993 proved to be a turning point in Jeff's career. He drove for several owners and won in Myrtle Beach, South Carolina, with Ward coming in second. Jeff drove a Ford and finished the Busch year with 28 starts, 1 win, 3 top-5s, 10 top-10s, and he placed 14th in the rankings.

The Busch Series is often called the "junior" series because the drivers who excel in it "graduate" to the most prestigious races, the Winston Cup Series.

Jeff made his NASCAR Winston Cup debut in 1993 in the inaugural race at Loudon, in which he qualified sixth. It was his only NASCAR Winston Cup race of the season, but he caught the eye of the Stavola brothers (Billy and Mickey Stavola), who signed him to their team. Although Jeff would be expected to work publicity spots, he would have regular sponsors. Jeff wouldn't have to spend as much time raising money, so he would have more time to concentrate on driving.

"I wasn't thinking about Winston Cup racing, I had all the car owner I could stand, and he'd had all of me he could stand, and my option was Winston Cup racing, and that's why I went Cup racing," Jeff told the *Richmond Times-Dispatch*. "I thought the Busch Series was perfect for me, and I enjoyed it and loved it and never really gave much thought to Winston Cup until I got into it."

Jeff wasn't the only one in his family headed for the Cup Series. Ward was going there, too.

ROOKIE OF THE YEAR

Despite the fact that Jeff had won four Grand National races and was fairly well-known by the time he entered the NASCAR Winston Cup Series, he was in awe of the series and a little "gun-shy," he said. "I didn't know anything, much less how these cars drove. I had only run one race," he told the press.

Jeff and Ward were both first-year drivers in the NASCAR Winston Cup Series in 1994. Jeff ran the full season for the Stavola brothers' team. Ward signed on with A. C. Dillard and was a regular test driver for Hoosier Tires at the time.

By March, Jeff had established himself as one of the year's toughest rookies. But he was anxious as he went into the Purolator 500 at Atlanta Motor Speedway in Georgia. It's the same speedway where, in 1992, his debut had ended in a crash after only three laps. This time rain had cancelled his test session.

Ward had won the Busch Grand National race at

Jeff has a quiet moment before the start of a race. Although he was the 1994 Rookie of the Year, Jeff later admitted that he felt nervous and inexperienced his first NASCAR season.

the track the year before. "This place had me scared to death," Jeff said. "I got a lot of help from Ward. He knows this track well."

By the race's midpoint, Jeff led the field by a half-lap. He led four times for 87 laps but eventually fell to fourth position after he made a pit stop following the third yellow flag. (A solid yellow flag signals the racers to slow down when the track is dangerous because of a crash, debris, slick fluids, or rain.)

Pit stops have won or lost many a race for drivers. At some tracks, the cars only need 15 seconds to complete a lap. Each second a car is in the pit means it's behind that many seconds on the track. That's why it's important that the driver and team are in contact through two-way radios. The driver can explain problems, and the crew chief can give advice and direction to the driver as well as inform him on strategy. As the driver pulls into the pit lane, each crew member has been assigned a specific task, so multiple jobs are completed at one stop.

The problem is that the two-way radios are monitored by fans and other teams. Strategies may be overheard. Also, if a driver stops and the race is called off because of rain, he can lose his position on the track. With a lower finish, he gets fewer points.

In September, disaster hit. Jeff was leading the Rookie of the Year race by 12 points over Joe Nemecheck as the two prepared for the Miller 400 at the Richmond International Raceway in Virginia. Then Jeff was disqualified from the race when a NASCAR inspector discovered holes about the size of quarters in the tops of three roll bars. The bars are welded together to form a protective cage around the

driver. Holes reduce the cage's ability to withstand impact, making the car less safe. They are drilled in the top of the safety cage to reduce weight, but they only save about one to two pounds and are a violation of NASCAR's safety regulations.

NASCAR kicked Jeff and the Stavola brothers' racing team out of the race and fined them $10,000, one of the biggest fines since Junior Johnson was kicked out of NASCAR in 1991.

Jeff, shaken and angry, said he wasn't aware of the holes. "You don't build anything when it comes to safety and then drill holes in it," he said. "I am one rookie who has made all the races . . . and to not make this race because

In NASCAR racing, skilled pit crews like this one are crucial to a driver's chances for victory. The driver and the crew chief must agree on a strategy, and the crew must be very fast and efficient.

of this is pretty hard to take."

By the end of his first full season in the Cup, Jeff had 30 starts, 2 top-5s, and 3 top-10s. He finished 24th in points. Above all else, in a year of talented rookies, he'd won the hotly contested battle for the 1994 MAXX Rookie of the Year title. During the season, he'd sometimes been chased by Joe Nemecheck and Steve Grissom and sometimes came in after his brother Ward, Mike Wallace, John Andretti, and Loy Allen Jr.

"We battled all year long to win that rookie thing. I kept telling everybody it didn't matter, but it does," Jeff admitted, adding, "One thing the rookie thing has taught us is the importance of consistency."

The 1995 season opened with great promise for the young driver, but it quickly began to crumble. In April, for the first time that season, Jeff failed to qualify for a race—the Hanes 500 at the Martinsville Speedway. Since his owners were too far down in points standings, Jeff did not receive one of the provisional starting points. Those went instead to Michael Waltrip, Derrike Cope, Geoffrey Bodine, and John Andretti.

In October, Ward won his first Winston Cup race. Ironically, up until this race, Jeff and Ward had had comparable careers, with both eventually winning in every series they'd competed in, but Jeff had always won in a series before Ward. This time, Ward had beaten Jeff to a first win, so Jeff felt even more pressure to collect his own victory.

Jeff stayed with the Stavola brothers for two years, but by the middle of 1995, it was clear that the team was consistently unable to run out in front and had settled back to mid-pack.

"I can point to several races we ran in the top 12 and didn't finish because we broke motors or something dumb happened. But the way we performed, I was not displeased whatsoever," Jeff said.

Also in 1995, Jeff and Kim's daughter, Kimberly Paige, was born, and Jeff let it be known that his family would always come first in his life.

When the 1995 season closed, Jeff was 32nd in points and had only 1 top-5 and 2 top-10s, a disappointing finish for the 1994 Rookie of the Year.

ROUSH SIGNS BURTON

Jack Roush, renowned owner of Roush Racing, had been watching Jeff for some time. Roush was looking for a driver for his new team. Jeff had discussed his interest in Roush's team with his longtime friend, Roush driver Mark Martin. Jeff felt he could work well with both Martin and Ted Musgrave, another Roush driver, but he had not considered himself to be in the running for the position.

Despite Jeff's ill-fated 1995 season, Roush made him an offer. Jeff liked the Stavola brothers, but going with Roush would give him a chance to reestablish himself. It could be a great career move.

In September 1995, Roush announced that Jeff would drive for his newly created third team. The team would be sponsored by Exide Batteries and be based in Charlotte, North Carolina, about an hour south of Roush's main base of operations in Liberty, North Carolina. Managing the operation would be legendary mechanic Buddy Parrott, who had won

Jack Roush (right), owner of Roush Racing, signed Jeff for his racing team in 1995. Here the two celebrate Jeff's win at the 1998 Jiffy Lube Miami 300.

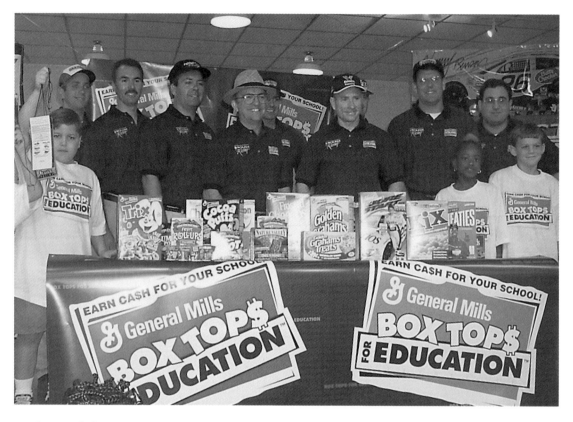

Jack Roush (in center with light hat), Mark Martin (on Roush's left), and other Roush Racing drivers appear at a promotional event. Jeff happily joined the top-notch team, believing he would have a better chance to win in the Winston Cup races.

18 races in two years with Rusty Wallace and had worked as crew chief for some of NASCAR's best drivers.

"We will rely more on Buddy to run a single car than we're currently relying on other people to run the others," Roush said.

Roush's two-car team of Martin and Musgrave would stay based in Liberty. This move gave Roush three separate Winston Cup contenders, and each had its own crew.

Jeff had just entered the newest phenomenon in the Winston Cup Series—multicar teams. At one time, such teams didn't exist, but by 1996 there were four multicar teams. Because NASCAR only allows each car seven testing sessions per season, one of the advantages of multicar teams is that they can share important information from their different test drives. In Roush's case, three teams meant a total of 21 test drives to learn from.

Some wondered if the third team felt at odds by being in a different location, but Jeff soon quashed that rumor. "I don't feel like, and nobody on this team feels like we are slighted anything by being the brand-new team. The advantage is that we had some people who were willing to help us get started and give us some information," Jeff told the *Detroit News*.

However, the Exide team didn't find a home in Charlotte. Instead, it set up north of Charlotte in Dick Moroso's shops in Mooresville, North Carolina. Jeff also moved his family from South Boston to North Carolina, to be closer to the shop.

When Jeff first rolled out the No. 99 Exide Batteries Ford Thunderbird in Daytona, he came out a strong contender for the Winston Cup. (Ward was now driving a Pontiac for Bill Davis.)

By the time Jeff reached his hometown track in South Boston, Virginia, he had finished 5th at Daytona and 13th at Rockingham. He probably had the fastest car in South Boston and led three times for 53 laps, nearly winning. He was in the lead when the caution flag waved on lap 350, but he took a pit stop. He was fifth out of the pits and rapidly passed Rusty Wallace, but he couldn't pass teammate Ted Musgrave. The Roush team finished with Musgrave in third, Jeff fourth, Martin fifth. Martin later said he fought off an urge to race three-wide (side by side) with his teammates.

After three races, Jeff was second in points going into Atlanta for the Purolator 500.

"There's a heck of a lot less pressure being second than being 32nd," he said. "This might sound a bit pretentious, but I really expected to run this well. Racing is not complicated: it's putting the right people on the right team and letting them get to work."

But Jeff's hopes were dashed when, in the final minutes before the end of the morning practice, his car gave off a puff of steam and slowed. It had overheated. The crew cooled the engine and tried without success to patch the car together. Jeff's chance of qualifying for one of the 38 starting positions was low, and he wasn't eligible for a provisional spot because his team was new.

Team officials and Ford representatives jumped into action, asking Ford teams with provisional opportunities to stand on the qualifying time, giving Jeff an opportunity to beat their first-round qualifying time. Junie Donlavey, owner of the Fords driven by Mike Wallace, asked him to stand on his time. Wallace agreed.

Jeff ran his lap at 30.346 seconds, but he couldn't beat Wallace's 30.221 seconds for the 38th position. The missed start dropped Jeff to 14th in points.

With tears in his eyes, Jeff tried to explain to his team the pain of not qualifying for the race. Had it happened one week later, his new team would have been eligible for a spot. "Obviously, it's devastating," he said later.

By the next race, Jeff was literally back on the track. He placed 10th at the TranSouth Financial 400 in Darlington. And he just kept on going.

Jeff poses with his wife and daughter after winning the CarsDirect.com 400. Jeff has always made it clear that his family is his first priority.

In August, Jeff was pleased but baffled after winning his first Winston Cup pole at the Goodwrench 400 at Michigan International Speedway in Brooklyn, Michigan. There he had also logged a career-high Championship Points Race finish of 13th.

"Winning the pole means a lot because it's where we've really struggled; it's been our weak link. When we didn't make the field in Atlanta, I told them [the crew] we'd sit on the

Jeff drove pickups like these in the 1996 Craftsman Truck Series. Although he did well in several races that year and went on to finish 13th in the Winston Cup season, his first win remained elusive.

pole somewhere this year. And, this is the same car we didn't make it [with] in Atlanta."

Also, during open dates in the Cup schedule in June 1996, Jeff competed in the NASCAR Craftsman Truck Series events. So did NASCAR Winston Cup Series champion Rusty Wallace. Both men were driving Ford pickups—Jeff for Roush Racing, Wallace for Penske South—and both were trying to qualify for the inaugural DeVilbiss SuperFinish 200 in late June at the Nazareth Speedway in Pennsylvania.

Both drivers made it to DeVilbiss, but neither won. Jeff started in 16th position and finished in 4th; Wallace started in 7th position and finished in 9th. At the end of the 1996 Craftsman Truck Series, Jeff ranked 42nd, with 4 starts,

1 top-5 and 3 top-10s.

Jeff returned to the Busch Series for his first race in that junior series since 1993. Like many of the Cup drivers, he was not actively seeking the Busch Series championship. He raced to gain publicity, to interest fans, and to learn the track before the next day's Cup race. In May, he competed at the Red Dog 300 at the Charlotte Motor Speedway in Concord, North Carolina. He started in 7th position but finished 42nd in the field because of mechanical problems.

When the Winston Cup Series season closed, Jeff was an impressive 13th in points, had 6 top-5s, 12 top-10s, and 1 pole, but he hadn't won a race. Would 1997 bring him a trip to Victory Lane?

WRECKS AND BREAKS

J eff entered the 1997 Winston Cup season as one of "the Underdogs," a select group of well-liked drivers who had been plagued with various problems in their quest for the Cup's championship. The esteemed group included John Andretti, Dave Marcis, Rick Mast, Kyle Petty, Darren Waltrip, and Michael Waltrip.

Impatient for a win, Jeff was anxious about the new season. But he needn't have worried; 1997 would prove to be Jeff's breakthrough year.

It started with the inaugural weekend of the Texas Motor Speedway outside Fort Worth, Texas. Rain fell heavily. Thursday's and Friday's qualifying rounds had been postponed, as had most of the practice sessions.

The track was besieged with problems. Water was oozing through holes onto the new track. Rain had caused potholes. There were concerns about the track's quad-oval design. Tempers were short. Spectators were muddy and wet but not complaining.

The design and condition of a speedway can be an important factor in winning or losing a race. In 1997 Jeff won at the Texas Motor Speedway after wrecks reduced the field to 27 cars.

Without a qualifying time to establish the starting grid, NASCAR had lined up the cars according to its standard procedure. The top 35 places were determined by Winston Cup points, and the last 8 were given in order of the postmarks on entries for the event.

It was a difficult track. Drivers were bewildered, owners frustrated, and both groups were uneasy. Their apprehension proved well-founded. By the end of the day, 8 of 10 yellow flags had flown because of wrecks, 21 cars were damaged or knocked out by accidents, and only 27 cars finished the 73 laps.

Jeff had an advantage. He'd been one of the few able to test drive before the rain, which meant he could tune his car's spring and shock selections to fit best with the Texas bowl.

Buddy Parrott was ready in the pits. In the ninth caution, 68 laps from the finish, Parrott called Jeff in for fuel.

"Some of the other leaders didn't come in until later in the caution. So that gave us track position. That's really what won the race for us," Jeff said.

After 96 starts in the Cup Series, Jeff had made it to Victory Lane.

Not everything went well that year. At the Michigan Speedway, Jeff Gordon lost control of his Chevrolet in turns three and four as he moved to the inside of Dale Earnhardt's Chevrolet. He spun in front of the Fords driven by Dick Trickle and Burton. Injured in the crash, which also took out primary cars for Gordon and Trickle for the Miller 400, Burton was taken to a hospital in Jackson, Michigan, and then released.

More than two weeks later, with bruises and

muscle strains mostly healed, Jeff's leg still hurt. He had an MRI (magnetic resonance imaging) done on his leg. It was broken.

Would Jeff be able to drive in July at Daytona?

Parrott quipped, "You don't put on the brakes at Daytona so he should be fine." He went on to explain that Jeff's broken leg hadn't bothered him in driving. "His [bruised] ribs were the big thing because driving the race car is a seat of the pants thing, and if you're favoring your ribs you can't hold the steering wheel just right like you need to." He added that the doctors had provided Jeff a brace for his leg.

Jeff finished the Daytona 400 in eighth position, but this time Ward was hospitalized with a concussion after a nine-car crack-up that took

Jeff's No. 99 car looks battered after a wreck during a 1999 race. At the Michigan Motor Speedway in 1997, Jeff broke his leg in a crash. But thanks to a brace, he was able to compete in the Daytona 500 only a few weeks later.

place when the judges lifted the caution flag with only one lap to go. The track was littered with car parts and debris as cars jockeyed for the winning position.

Jeff took home his second career Cup victory at the New Hampshire International Speedway that same month. A gap of almost five seconds separated him from Dale Earnhardt's Chevrolet.

"I got a hell of a race team," Jeff said. "It's only a year and a half we've been together, and to get two wins and be as competitive as we are says a lot about this team."

At an average speed of 117.194 mph, Jeff also broke Jeff Gordon's 1995 record of 107.029 mph.

By August, a rivalry was developing between Jeff and Gordon. At Darlington, Jeff's temper flared as he traded paint with Gordon in their charge for first- and second-place finishes.

Gordon recalled later that he saw Jeff coming and moved down because Jeff was making a run on him. "He plowed into the back of me and almost lifted the wheels off the ground. My car kind of took off sideways. I don't think he was expecting that. It knocked him onto the apron," Gordon described.

Jeff had his side of the story. "I got under him and he cut me down," he told *Winston Cup Illustrated.* "I turned right on him because he turned left. I just didn't get him good enough. I thought [Dale] Jarrett was going to win the race, but I was going to do my best to make sure he [Gordon] didn't win the race because he cut down on me."

Burton added, "I would have got him, but I got the toe-in knocked out when we hit. . . . I tried to put him in the wall and I just missed him. . . . He

[was] going for a million dollars. You can't blame him, but I'm going for a win, too, and I was going to do whatever I had to. I had him passed."

Gordon got his million. Jeff got second place.

In early September, Jeff had to hand the wheel over to relief driver Todd Bodine. An inner ear infection, which caused him to lose his balance and feel dizzy, sidelined him. Since he'd completed 68 laps in the New Hampshire, NASCAR rules allowed Jeff to gain points from Bodine's run. The No. 99 ended up 14th, and Jeff kept his 4th-place spot in the points race. The ear problem kept him from the qualifying rounds in Dover, too. But he took a provisional spot and ended the race 11th.

By late September, Jeff was fully recovered. He charged to his third career Cup victory at

Jeff (No. 99 at right) almost touches Jeff Gordon as he edges into the lead, and the win, at the 1998 Select Batteries 400. During the 1997 season, the two Jeffs began quite a rivalry, often trading first- and second-place finishes.

Crew chief Frank Stoddard is in constant touch with Jeff during a race. Stoddard, Jeff, and the crew have worked hard to become a winning team.

Martinsville Speedway after NASCAR took the rare step of levying a stop-and-go penalty on leader Rusty Wallace.

Wallace had jumped ahead on consecutive restarts late in the race. The penalty dropped Wallace from 1st to 15th. Wallace claimed he never jumped the restart because he was the leader. NASCAR officials said the proper place for a restart is the gate at the exit of turn four, but Wallace accelerated about 100 feet from the crossover. A spokesman for NASCAR said the team had received two warnings about jumping the restart.

Jeff won, but only after Bobby Hamilton gave him a battle. Hamilton pushed the nose of his Pontiac ahead of Jeff's Ford. With Jeff on the outside groove, they battled side by side for about six laps. Finally, the No. 99 got in front of the pesky Pontiac. In the end, Jeff posted a 0.778-second victory over Dale Earnhardt, who had passed Hamilton with only five laps to go.

It was a day of success for the Burton family: Ward had taken the pole, and Jeff had won the race.

Jeff exploded into the top ranks of the Cup Series in 1997. He ended the year 4th in points, with 32 starts, 3 wins, 13 top-5s, and 18 top-10s. Also in the Busch Series, he had 13 starts, 2 wins, 9 top-5s, 10 top-10s, one pole, and was 26th in points.

Jeff had now won races in every type of series he had entered, but despite his successes, he didn't celebrate. He firmly believes doing so is inviting big trouble. He fears success might make him content and that contentment might ruin his edge on the track.

As the season drew to a close, Roush Racing moved from a three-car team to a five-car team and announced that Parrott, who'd overseen only Jeff's car in 1997, would be team manager for both Jeff's and Martin's cars. Martin's team would be housed in the same shop. Jimmy Flennig would continue as Martin's crew chief, but Jeff would enter the 1998 season with a new crew chief, Frank Stoddard.

In 1998, one journalist wrote, "If Jeff Gordon had never been born, we'd all be talking about Jeff Burton right now." Jeff was that good, but to win the championship, his new team would need to meld together fast. He was again poised to be a championship contender and debuted the new No. 99—a Ford Taurus.

The year didn't start well. The crew suffered engine problems that put them out of two races. On two occasions, wrecks cut their days short. Problems in the pits and in pole qualifying plagued the team all year.

The Exide team's pit stops improved dramatically over the course of the year, as did the adjustments they made to the car. Jeff and Stoddard were quickly becoming a powerful team.

At the New Hampshire International Speedway in July, Jeff made his first trip of the season to Victory Lane. Of the final 221 laps, Jeff had led all but 30.

Jeff was sure he was the car to beat after his final pit stop. "You know four laps into a run if you've got what it takes or not. . . . I said, 'Man, we've got it made. Don't wreck, don't miss a shift, don't do something stupid, and we'll win this race.'"

"Nobody could touch [Burton]," said Jeff Gordon, who came in third. "He definitely was in a different league than the rest of us."

It's Jeff's favorite track on the circuit. "I prefer this track over the rest because I have competed in every Winston Cup race there and have won in two divisions, Winston Cup and Busch Grand National," he explained.

The team kept going strong, finishing in the top-10 in five out of the next seven races. By the fall race at Richmond International Raceway, they had pooled their talents and become a winning team.

Jeff dominated the field during most of the race at Richmond. He led six times for a total of 203 laps, but with 10 laps to go, rival Gordon caught up with him. In a side-by-side battle, they ran down the stretch toward the checkered flag. Jeff was in the high groove and

Gordon in the low groove. It was the last caution of the race that decided Jeff's destiny.

"We caught that caution just right and had an awesome stop. We were in trouble on the long runs," Jeff said. The caution set up the short run to the finish. Gordon came in second.

Despite some problems, Jeff finished the year with a Winston Cup career high of $2,626,987 in winnings. He had 33 starts, 18 top-5s, and 23 top-10s—more than all but two drivers. Jeff won twice but finished fifth in the final standings—one point short of his fourth position in 1997. Still, it had been a remarkable year. In the Busch Series, he had 13 starts, 3 victories, 7 top-5 finishes, 9 top-10s, 2 poles, and finished 30th in points.

Jeff drove into 1999 as a man growing accustomed to winning.

A ROLLER-COASTER YEAR

In 1999, the racer to beat was Jeff Gordon. He was after his third Winston Cup championship in a row and his fourth overall. To compete successfully against Gordon, Jeff would have to improve his qualifying, be consistent, and finish more races than in 1998. As the season began, he felt ready.

"At some point in your career, you have to get over that potential label and start doing it," Jeff said.

And like all the Winston Cup contenders at the season opening at Daytona, Jeff hoped 1999 would be his year to be the Winston Cup Series champion. Many thought he'd make it, too. He was calmer, took losses better, and had learned to work well within the Roush organization and with his crew. And his working partnership with Mark Martin was expanding onto the track.

Jeff (front row, second from right) and his brother Ward (front row, far right) pose with six other NASCAR drivers (back row, from left to right: Rusty Wallace, Dale Jarrett, Dale Earnhardt, and Dale Earnhardt Jr.; front row, first and second from left: Mark Martin and Bobby Labonte) at the Talladega Superspeedway. Each driver won a race in the 2000 season, marking the first time that eight different drivers had wins in the first eight races of the season.

"It's a strain, obviously, when you have two competitive teams. So we just work extra hard to make sure everybody knows that we have the same opportunities," Jeff told *USA Today.* Martin commented, "[Burton] has the personality that makes the deal work."

Jeff left Daytona with a disappointing DNF (did not finish) after a 12-car chain-reaction crash between turns three and four on lap 135. Dale Jarrett's No. 88 had been tapped by another car and spun sideways. It went down onto the apron, and came back across the track, then was hit and turned upside down. The crash took out the cars of Jeff Burton, Mark Martin, Joe Nemecheck, Geoffrey Bodine, and Elliott Sander, among others.

As expected, Gordon won both the race and the pole.

But at the Las Vegas Motor Speedway, Jeff made it to Victory Lane, and Ward was right by his side. For four laps around the 1.5-mile track, the brothers dueled for the lead, racing side by side as Jeff tried to take over Ward's Pontiac. As he was going into the second turn on the 257th lap of the 267-lap event, Jeff slipped around the outside of Ward's car. He then began pulling away and won the race by 1.074 seconds.

"I tried to crowd Jeff as much as I could in the exit corner, but I couldn't wreck my brother," Ward recalled.

Jeff admitted, "I kind of giggled in the race car because Winston Cup racing is a really big deal, and for two brothers to be racing for a win in one of the biggest races of the year, that's pretty special."

At the Atlanta Motor Speedway in Georgia,

Gordon won, and Jeff dropped to fourth position, only to shoot back to win the rain-shortened race at Darlington, which was called after lap 164 of the 293-lap event. Gordon had won the pole, but he came in third.

Neither Gordon nor Jeff would win the next four races, but at the California Speedway, Gordon came in first, Jeff second. The war of the Jeffs was heating up, and NASCAR fans loved it.

"My way of racing is that you just run as hard as you can all the time," Jeff told the

Jeff displays his $1 million bonus check for winning the Pepsi Southern 500 at the Darlington Speedway in 1995. Alongside is Phyllis Farmer, the fan who also won $1 million by picking Jeff as the winner.

Charlotte Observer. "What [Gordon] does such a good job of is playing 'possum'; you don't ever know if he can't run or if he's not running. He might be able to run faster than you, but he doesn't let you know until it's too late for you to do anything about it."

Gordon took the pole at Richmond in the spring, but he came in 31st to Jeff's 37th-place finish. In the Winston at Lowe's Motor Speedway, Gordon came in third, and Jeff wrecked.

At the same speedway a week later, Bobby Labonte was the one to beat, and he had taken the pole.

Then there was the $1 million bonus that Labonte, Jeff, Ward, Gordon, and Mike Skinner had all earned a chance at in the No Bull 5. But to get it, they had to win the race. On that May weekend, it was a very close race that would be won in the final pit stops.

Interestingly, both Labonte and Jeff were facing the same problems in the corners as they went into the final 30 laps. The question to each crew was whether to tighten or loosen the car. If a car is "tight," the front of the car wants to go to the outside wall and not turn into the corner. If a car is "loose," the rear of the car wants to slide out and go toward the outside wall.

Labonte's crew added an extra pound of air pressure in his tires to help *loosen* his car for the final 30 laps. Stoddard chose to make a lot of adjustments to Jeff's No. 99 and to *tighten* the stock car. Stoddard had felt it was too loose to run with Labonte's, so the crew adjusted the car for a 30-lap run, not a 70-lap run. It was a risky move. Afraid the plan might be overheard and tip their hand, Stoddard and Jeff didn't use radio communications.

"I wasn't sure we had made the right moves," Stoddard admitted later.

On the final pit stop, Jeff's time was 17.3 seconds; Labonte's 17.4. Out of the pits, Jeff took the lead, but Labonte took it over on lap 381. Jeff pushed the No. 99's throttle harder, and three laps later he was in the lead. Labonte closed the gap to 0.574 seconds, but he couldn't overtake Jeff. Gordon had trouble with handling and finished 39th.

It was Jeff's third win of the season and eighth career victory in the Cup. He had won the $1 million bonus and was ahead in points.

Gordon took the pole in June at the Michigan Speedway, but Jarrett won. Gordon came in second, Jeff third, and Ward fourth.

At the Pocono 500, Labonte won, and Gordon was second. Jeff crossed the finish line in 36th place with the cars after him all out because of accidents or engine problems. Gordon took both the pole and race at the Sears Point Raceway in Sonoma, California, one of only two road racing venues in Winston Cup. Jeff finished 24th after his gearbox broke entering turn 11. And at the Daytona 400, Jeff came in 3rd, Gordon 21st.

Jeff moved into the lead at the NHIS 300 after rookie Tony Stewart ran out of fuel just two laps before he would likely have taken his first Cup victory.

With 10 laps to go, Stoddard pitted Jeff for the quickest pit stop of the day—three seconds. Jeff, who had started in 38th position, won the race. Stoddard's fuel strategy had worked. The rival Jeffs were neck and neck with four

Sometimes racing has its light moments. Here Jeff (right) and Bobby LaBonte dress up as Wayne and Garth, characters from the movie Wayne's World, *in a Coca-Cola promotion.*

victories each.

Gordon had taken the pole and placed third in the race. After having led the race for 103 laps, rookie Tony Stewart finished 10th and stormed out of the track. He later apologized.

Jeff Gordon came back to win the pole at the Indianapolis Motor Speedway in Indiana and then came in third, with Jeff in fifth and Ward in sixth. Gordon went on to win at the fall Watkins Glen International in New York, where Jeff came in 13th.

Ward took the pole at the Michigan Speedway 400, but Labonte won the race. Gordon came in 2nd, and Jeff was in 37th—after a wreck in which Tony Stewart passed and clipped the

No. 99, sending it to the wall. At the Bristol Motor Speedway in Tennessee, Gordon was 4th and Jeff, 17th.

The odds of winning two Cup races at the same track in the same year aren't good. They are even worse if both races are rain-shortened. But Jeff did just that with his win at the Southern 500 at Darlington, the oldest super-speedway event.

"Deciding whether to pit or not to pit for tires [after the second red flag] was really, really stressful," he said. "I figured there was no way it could [end in the rain] twice in one year."

Ward was second behind his brother. Gordon finished 13th. Jeff also collected a second $1 million bonus, as did a lucky fan who had picked Jeff as the winner. Jeff and Gordon were now tied, each with five wins. But neither won a Cup event for several races afterward.

By the September race at NHIS, the racers and crews were tired. It was the seventh race of 12 straight race weekends. Rain caused the cancelation of the practice and pole qualifying.

"This is a grueling schedule," Jeff told the *Boston Herald*. "It's a physically and mentally hard time of the year because we run so many races in a row. You can utilize this day to get everybody a little rest and to spend a little time talking about something other than rear ends and transmissions and springs and shocks."

Then Gordon broke through. He won the Martinsville 500, with Jeff placing 9th, and the following week's Lowes Motor Speedway 500, where Jeff placed 37th. That would be Gordon's last trip to Victory Lane for the season.

Jeff, though, would win one more race in 1999, the Rock's 400. For the third time during the 1999 season, Ward came in second.

At the end of the Winston Cup season, Gordon had won seven races to Jeff's six. In the Cup standings, for the second year, Jeff came in fifth, with 4,733 points; Gordon finished sixth with 4,620 points. Jeff had three DNFs and six finishes outside of the top 30. His inconsistency had kept him on a roller coaster and cost him the Cup.

In the Busch standings Jeff started 14 times—less than half the starts of the winner— and had 1 win, 7 top-5s, and 12 top-10s. He ended the season with 2,091 points.

"It was an up-and-down year for us," Jeff told *NASCAR Online*. "We're proud of our six wins but we're disappointed at the number of races we didn't finish. To be a champion you have to be competitive in every race. We had some mechanical failures, and I made some mistakes. If you want to be competitive you can't do that."

In August 1999, Jack Roush extended the contracts of Jeff and Mark Martin, his two top drivers, through the 2005 season. The agreement positioned Jeff so that he could remain a part of Roush Racing beyond his driving career. The contract gave him the flexibility to retire anytime he wants, although he doesn't expect to retire in the near future.

In 2000, the No. 99 debuted with a new paint scheme and graphics. While the original colors of black, silver, and pink were still used, the hood was now white, lightning bolt graphics decorated the doors, and royal blue was added to the front portion of the car.

The car may have looked different, but the 2000 season began with now-familiar success. At

*Jeff Burton looks determined
to continue his winning ways
in 2000 and beyond.*

the Daytona 500 on February 20, Jeff finished
in second place behind Dale Jarrett. Nine races
into the year, he sat in fifth position in the Cup
standings, 134 points behind leader and fellow
Roush driver Mark Martin. In those nine races,
Jeff had won $2,870,209.

He had 5 top-5 finishes, including a win in
the CarsDirect.com 400 at the Las Vegas Motor
Speedway on March 5. He added second-place
finishes in both the DIRECTV 500 at the Texas
Motor Speedway on April 2 and the Goody's
Body Pain 500 at Martinsville Speedway on
April 9.

Ward was off to a solid start as well. He won
the Mall.com 400 at the Darlington Raceway on
March 19 and came in third in the Food City 500
at Bristol Motor Speedway the following week.

After nine races, Ward sat in third position in the Cup standings.

Jeff remains eager to greet the millennium as one of the top contenders in the Winston Cup Series. But he and his team recognize the importance of increasing their consistency. Poor starting positions make it harder to perform well on race day, a fact that was brought home to them in the DieHard 500 at Talladega Superspeedway on April 16. Jeff worked the No. 99 up to a 12th-place finish, but the car started in only 38th. They all understand that everyone will need to work hard as a team to bring the coveted championship home.

"We've learned a lot from 1999," he said. "We're not competing against Jeff Gordon or Dale Jarrett or Mark Martin. We work hard every week to do the best that we can. If we do that and get some breaks, then who knows?"

Will Jeff win a Winston Cup championship in the 21st century? As he put it, "What kind of a driver and team player would I be if I didn't think we had a good chance to win the championship going into every season?"

CHRONOLOGY

1967   Born on June 29 in South Boston, Virginia.

1974   Begins racing go-karts at the local track, South Boston Speedway.

1984   Has first stock car victory at South Boston Speedway.

1986   Becomes the youngest driver in NASCAR history to win a late-model stock car race.

1987   Is track cochampion at Orange County Speedway in Virginia.

1988   Voted most popular driver at South Boston Speedway.

1989   Runs first full season in the NASCAR Busch Grand National.

1990   Wins his first Busch race at Martinsville Speedway; continues to get one win a year in the Busch Series in South Boston, 1991.

1993   Enters his first Winston Cup Series race at the New Hampshire International Speedway, qualifying for sixth position; joins the Stavola brothers' team.

1994   Receives NASCAR Winston Cup's Rookie of the Year award.

1995   Signs on late in the year with Roush Racing.

1996   Wins his first Winston Cup pole at Michigan International Speedway and finishes the season 13th in points—a career high; races in both the Busch and Winston Cup Series.

1997   Has his first career win in the Winston Cup Series at the Texas Motor Speedway; wins two more events in the Winston Cup; finishes the season with a career-high fourth in points.

1998   Finishes the year with a career high in winnings and fifth in the final standings; has 2 wins, 18 top-5s, 23 top-10s—more than all but two other drivers.

1999   Finishes fifth in the standings; extends his contract with Roush Racing through 2005.

2000   Takes second at the Daytona 500; wins the CarsDirect.com 400 at the Las Vegas Motor Speedway.

STATISTICS

NASCAR WINSTON CUP SERIES

YEAR	RACES	WINS	TOP 5	TOP 10	POLES	EARNINGS	POINT STANDINGS
1993	1	0	0	0	0	$9,550	-
1994	30	0	2	3	0	$594,700	24th
1995	29	0	1	2	0	$630,770	32nd
1996	30	0	6	12	1	$884,303	13th
1997	32	3	13	18	0	$2,296,614	4th
1998	33	2	18	23	0	$2,626,987	5th
1999	34	6	18	23	0	$5,725,399	5th
2000*	10	1	5	6	0	$2,870,209	5th
Career	**199**	**12**	**63**	**87**	**1**	**$15,638.532**	

*as of April 16, 2000

FURTHER READING

Assael, Shaun. *Wide Open: Days and Nights on the NASCAR Tour.* New York: Ballantine Books, 1998, 1999 (with updated forward by the author).

Burt, William M. *Behind the Scenes of NASCAR Racing.* Osceola, WI: Motorbooks International, 1997.

Girdler, Allan. *Stock Car Racers: The History and Folklore of NASCAR's Premier Series: "Tail Straight Out and Belly to the Ground."* Osceola, WI: Motorbooks International, 1988.

Mooney, Loren. *A Kids' Guide to NASCAR.* New York: Sports Illustrated for Kids, 1999.

Moriarty, Frank. *The Encyclopedia of Stock Car Racing.* New York: Metro Books, 1998.

Schaller, Bob. *Top Stars of NASCAR.* Vol. 1. Grand Island, NE: Cross Training Publishing, 1999.

ABOUT THE AUTHOR

June Ford is a nationally published writer and ghostwriter. She is a former journalist and newspaper and magazine editor. June has written, edited, proofread, and coordinated projects for national and regional publishing houses and magazines. Since 1987, she has owned and operated her own company, JFE Editorial Services. She is a writer-in-residence for the state of Texas. June has a bachelor's degree from Texas Christian University in Fort Worth, Texas.

PHOTO CREDITS:
ALLSPORT/Craig Jones: 2; ALLSPORT USA/Jonathan Ferrey: 6; Ai Wire/Vern Verna: 8, 26, 53; AP/Wide World Photos/Karl DeBlack: 9; AP/Wide World Photos/Robert Willett: 10; NMI: 14, 17, 22, 29, 38, 40; NASCAR/NMI: 21; NEWSMAKERS/Michael Allen: 32; PRN/NMI: 34, 56; NEWSMAKERS/Robert Laberge: 37; Reuters/Mike Tussing: 43; UPI/John C. Anderson: 45; UPI/ Roger Williams: 46; NASCAR/Nigel Kinrade: 50; UPI/Lee K. Marriner: 59.

INDEX